ENDORSEMENT

Super salute to Bruce. Before attending his workshop, I left a lot of deals on the table. After attending his workshop, Bruce armed me with better questions to ask & now I have the confidence needed to ask the questions necessary to close more deals. If you're unsure of how to ask better questions & how to find the right people to ask, attend Bruce's workshop ASAP. I'm very excited to implement this information & execute. Thank you Bruce !

Rafaniel Jimerson - Founder of Stamper Signings LLC

BETTER QUESTIONS

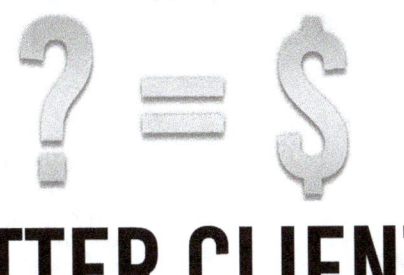

BETTER CLIENTS

How to Attract and Keep Clients Through Clarity, Confidence and Effective Communication

BRUCE HILL

FOREWORD BY DR. AJITA M. ROBINSON

WWW.TRUEVINEPUBLISHING.ORG

Better Questions, Better Clients
By Bruce Hill

Published by
True Vine Publishing Co.
810 Dominican Dr.
Nashville, TN 37228
www.TrueVinePublishing.org

Printed in the United States of America—First printing.

FOREWORD BY
DR. AJITA ROBINSON

It's often said that the right people come into your life at the right time, and my introduction to Bruce is a perfect testament to that truth. We met through a mutual friend when I was searching for someone who could support my clients—mental health therapists who had built their careers around healing and serving others. But when it came to building sustainable businesses, many of them were struggling.

You see, therapists are often taught to devalue their services, believing their work should be freely given rather than fairly compensated. They're rarely taught how to sell, and when the concept of sales does come up, it's often met with discomfort and resistance. But I knew that in order to help them create lasting impact, I needed someone who could reframe what selling truly means.

Enter Bruce.

From the moment we connected, I knew he was different. Bruce doesn't view sales as a transactional exchange—he sees it as an opportunity to serve. His unwavering belief that "selling is serving" resonated deeply with me. He understood the heart of what therapists do and why it matters. More importantly, he shared my values around valuing people over profits and building a living legacy.

Bruce has an extraordinary way of making sales feel natural, aligned, and even joyful. Through his guidance, my clients have gained clarity around their offers, confidently communicated their value, and embraced pricing that reflects the worth of their expertise. He has shown them that selling is not about convincing someone to buy but about offering a solution that genuinely serves a need.

His signature 4P Framework is a game-changer. By focusing on People, Promise, Process, and Pricing, Bruce equips entrepreneurs to navigate sales conversations with confidence and authenticity. The therapists I serve have experienced incredible transformations under his mentorship. They're no longer hesitant to advocate for their businesses because they understand that their services change lives.

One of the greatest gifts Bruce offers is his unwavering belief in people. He understands that behind every service offered, there is a story. Behind every client, there is a desire for change. And behind every sale, there is an opportunity to create lasting impact. Through his 4P Framework, Bruce has distilled years of experience into actionable insights that make sales feel natural, intentional, and, dare I say, enjoyable.

But beyond the strategies and frameworks, what really sets Bruce apart is his heart. He is a giver, a servant leader, and a relentless champion of others. He pours into others, offering wisdom and encouragement without hesitation. His passion for helping others succeed is evident in every conversation, every training, and now, in every word of this book. You are not simply reading a sales manual—you are receiving the culmination of wisdom from someone who genuinely cares about your success.

As you read through these pages, prepare to experience a shift. Prepare to challenge old beliefs and embrace a new perspective. Whether you're a business owner, a consultant, or someone navigating the world of sales for the first time, Bruce's insights will help you unlock the confidence to sell with purpose. Because when selling becomes serving, the impact you create will ripple far beyond the walls of your business.

Here's to asking better questions, serving with purpose, and saying "yes" to the incredible possibilities ahead.

It's an honor to call Bruce a friend and a colleague. I'm so grateful you get to learn from him, too.

With admiration and gratitude,

Dr. Ajita M. Robinson

TABLE OF CONTENTS

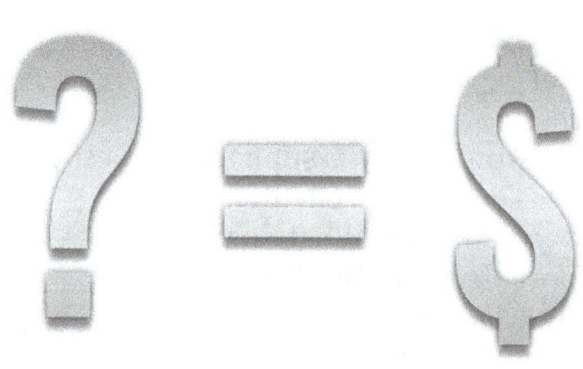

INTRODUCTION

The questions you are not asking are costing you money.

Whether you're a business owner, customer success manager, account executive, people leader, or entrepreneur wearing multiple hats the quality of your decisions depend on the quality of your questions.

You don't need to implement artificial intelligence, expensive software or even a complicated sales methodology. You need to ask better questions.

I wrote this book for you.

I wrote this book because the next level of your success is just a few questions away.

Your next investor.

Your next dream client.

Your next brilliant hire.

I interviewed dozens of founders, customer success leaders, and entrepreneurs to bring you a resource that will help attract and keep more clients.

From Baltimore, Maryland to Nashville, Tennessee. From Dubai, Nigeria, and the United Kingdom.

I want to thank each for their support of this project and for being part of making it a success. Look for their names in the Special Thanks section at the beginning of this book.

Some of the concepts you will be familiar with. There will be a few Ah-ha moments. But the biggest breakthrough is not inside this book. It is in the execution.

I am confident that applying the lessons learned will create a success story—I can't wait to hear it!

To supplement the contents of this book I created the Better Questions Toolkit. Use this as a simple how to and resource guide.

Scan the QR Code use code book

WHAT IS THE 4P FRAMEWORK?

Four simple questions. One focus. It is the answer to the question: "How do we attract and keep the type of clients we love to work with?"

There are four areas to the framework. People, Promise, Process, and Pricing. I have found these to be the most basic starting point for asking better questions. Each of these is foundational to your success in any area of your business.

I call it the 4P Framework.

This is not sales training. This is a clarity exercise. When used effectively, it results in a higher level of clarity internally within your team. Externally, your message becomes clearer, concise, and compelling. The result is hearing yes more often from investors, clients, and new hires.

In this section, I will walk you through each of the Ps (People, Promise, Process, and Pricing) and share how you can incorporate this strategy to help you achieve your goals as a business owner, entrepreneur, people leader, etc. The order of the framework is intentional, each building on the next to create clarity and build strategy. You'll be able to drive revenue and improve retention simply by asking better questions.

The goal of the 4P Framework is to simplify your decision-making. As a result, it becomes easier to achieve goals, and less time is wasted in trial and error. Focusing on the right actions yields the right results.

We will cover each of the 4Ps from two perspectives: external and internal. For the purposes of this discussion, we will use the following definition:

Internal customers = employees; those we hire, including employees, team members, vendors, and collaboration partners.

External customers = clients, those who hire us. They are those you serve or hope to serve as clients and future clients.

I will spend a brief amount of time on the 4P Framework, a portion of the time on tools and the majority of the time on it's application.

Now that we have that foundation, let's get started!

_____

_____

_____

_____

_____

_____

_____

_____

_____

_____

_____

_____

_____

_____

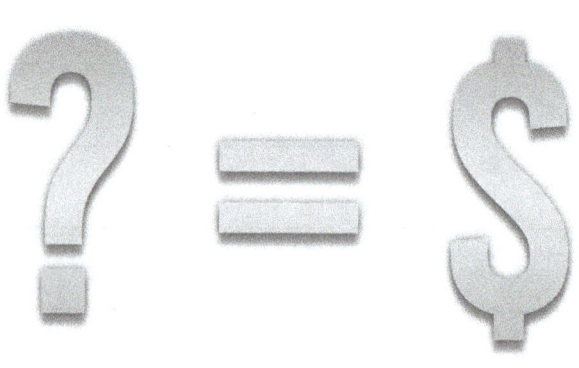

PEOPLE – WHO CAN WE SERVE WITH EXCELLENCE?

Internal Customers

One of my mentors, Dr. David Twilly, told me, "Bruce, the only business is people."

One of the first things I recommend is asking, "How do we grow our business from the inside out?" Before you hire a consultant or download the software to implement artificial intelligence, what questions do you need to ask? I believe the questions we were not asking are costing us money. This is true for all relationships.

As I thought about Dr. Twilly's statement, I began to understand what he meant. Why are people so important in business? Because of their impact on the business. We hear the intellects and techies talking about artificial intelligence, and everything could eventually be run by AI—a whole business from top to bottom, even sweeping the floors. The reality is that people will always be needed. How people operate a business will change. How to future-proof your business starts with your people. So, why not look at your greatest asset as the means of growing your business? In other words, if you take care of your people, you're taking care of your business. As you grow your people, you grow your business. And as I stated earlier, I want to provide you with the tools to invest in your business, which means investing in training in your most valuable asset, including teaching them this concept of asking better questions using the 4P Framework. Unfortunately, when leaders, owners, and entrepreneurs are looking at ways of growing or expanding a business, it's the people who are often taken for granted.

So, let's start with the internal customers. If you have asked the question, "How do we grow the business?" Your next question should be, "Who do we need to win?" This question is only part of the puzzle, but because it is open-ended, it sets the stage for determining how the right people are evaluated and hired.

Another way to approach this is by asking: What do we need to get done?

I did the 4P Framework exercise with my friend, who owns a staffing agency. He outsources executive assistants, so I asked him a few simple questions.

"Why did you decide to do this?" He said, "It helped me scale my business and eventually exit."

"How did an executive assistant help you to exit?" He told me it was about time. He was able to focus on his area of expertise and produce a higher quality of work because he wasn't spread thin. Better work got done faster. Because he wasn't the one doing everything, it eliminated the bottleneck. He realized he didn't sell executive assistants. He sold time freedom. His marketing changed. Who he reaches out to has changed. His new business is growing great! That is the power of better questions.

So, we have asked the question of who and how. The next logical question is, "What do we need to do to attract and keep good people?"

This always leads to another great question. What's our company culture? The word culture has become a little bit cliche. If you ask five people how you would describe the culture, you would probably get five different answers. But what kind of culture do we want to have? Although this seems like a simple question, it is the follow-up questions that will determine what you need to do to create the right environment into which you can attract and retain your internal customers— your employees.

What do we need to create this culture?

How do we get the internal team involved in their own success?

If you don't have any team members yet, consider this question again: "Who do we need to win?"

More than skills, "Who do we like to work with?

I did a project for a **startup. The founders were outdoors people, so they** mostly attracted outdoor people. But when they asked a different question, they got a different answer: "Who do we want to win with us?"

When they gave themselves an honest answer, they found a disconnect. They then helped everyone get on the same page—hire for more than skill and seek alignment on your vision, mission, and values.

Ultimately, it is about priorities. I'm not telling you to hire only one person. In some cases, this will be disastrous. But this question helps you prioritize: Who should be hired? It's a mental thought exercise to help you win. If we only hired one person, who would have the most positive impact? Who would help us quickly achieve results? How will they contribute to or impact success? Again, the question is the answer. **By asking better questions, we will undoubtedly get better answers (clients, employees, etc.).**

These are the same questions I asked myself. I had two roles I needed to fill, so I partnered with a local university to hire interns. I decided to pay a small salary, which was NOT required by the university. I thought about what I hoped to accomplish. I decided I wanted good people. We will ignore for a moment why internships should always be paid. I want to find people who believe in the mission. I asked myself, how can I make it easy for those people to decide to work with me and pay them well?

Of course, compensation of these internal customers is an entire conversation in and of itself, requiring a costing or salary analysis. But the idea is that if we want the best people, and you are following the model of taking care of your people, you will have to ask the sometimes tough questions of yourself or the company. What is the best compensation package I can offer them? Remember, if you are taking care of your people, they will take care of the business.

As an aside on this topic of compensation and hiring, it is important to note that if employees have to work several jobs to make ends meet, their attention and energy are split. If they are offered the same work but at higher pay, will they leave? What reason are you giving them to stay beyond their salary? This isn't only about money. People deserve to be treated well and paid well. Better people give us the best chance of success.

So, what can we do to attract the best people? Who do we need right now? What skills or experience can push us towards our next level of growth?

These are all open-ended questions that, when asked, will guide you to attracting and retaining the right people for your business growth.

External Customers

You may hear the term ICP, an ideal client profile. You may use the word customer. You might hear customer avatar. I have used target buyer. Those are good concepts, but when speaking about better clients, we should really be asking, Who can we serve with excellence?

No matter what you call them, the bigger question is, who are the clients you dream about?

The answer to that question is the difference between a good month and a record-breaking month. These are the people who refer you and are excited to tell other people about it. They leave you a five-star review.

They're the ones that are going to help you create success in your business. I do not want you crippled by the trap of "We help everyone." There are many people you can serve, but only a comparative few you can **serve with excellence**.

For example, we serve SaaS companies. Good, keep going. We serve SaaS companies in the health space. You're getting warmer. Let's say health tech spaces that are pre-seed or seed funding less than 100 employees. DING. You nailed it. Will other customers reach out to you? Yes, if you can serve them well, then accept their business. When you focus clearly on who you can serve with excellence, everything else is extra.

I want this WHO to be clear; I should be able to write it down in two or three sentences. I should be able to hand it to anyone, even a stranger on the street, and assuming they speak the same language, they can find those people for me. That's how clear I need to be.

Here's another question.

Did you choose those people as your ideal clients or better clients because that's what you wanted? Because that's the feedback your customers provide? If you don't have any customers, this might be a difficult answer. You will find additional resources at the end of this book to help you get more customers: "Turning Problems into Payments."

Remember, everything in business starts with people. So, who can we serve with excellence?

_____

_____

_____

_____

_____

_____

_____

_____

_____

_____

_____

_____

_____

_____

_____

PROMISE - WHAT IS THE TRANSFORMATION TO THEIR LIFE OR BUSINESS?

People, especially sales trainers, talk about solving the problem. Many sales trainers talk about the problem separate from the customer you are looking for. This is useful but overemphasized. What I discovered is that the problem is part of the identity of the person you're working with.

Let's look at an example. You're a fitness instructor who focuses on high school students. You don't want just any high school student. Chess club members may not be your target. You want high school students who are underperforming in their sport. The pain comes from making it to the championship game and losing. That's a good place to start, but too many get stuck there. We want to focus on the promise to identify those high school students who will become better (best) clients.

Here are some questions that are going to help you focus on the problem and the promise.

- Where are you going?
- What does success look like?
- What are the goals, vision, or mission?
- What is the desired future outcome?

Notice something really important. These are open-ended questions. They start with who, what, where, when, why, and how. Each is focused on the future—the future is why they want to work with you.

People with specific problems are among those we survey when identifying potential or future clients. The question we must ask is: Where do they end up as a result of working with us? That promise should lead to many more great questions.

- How are we going to do that?
- What does it look like?
- What does it mean?

We need to serve people where they are. Our goal is to help them toward where they want to go. That's the promise—the transformation we provide. This is the reason people pay for service. They do not know how to accomplish their goal and pay for your help. They may not want to do the work themselves, or they do not have the resources.

There are three resources: knowledge, tools, and time. If they don't know how, then they need you to teach them. If they lack the tools, you can equip them. If they are short on time, you can be their guide, or, alternatively, you can do it for them.

Let me tell you about the time I hired a graphic designer. Sure, I could have done it myself, but it would have taken a long time and been terrible. The cost and time of learning the skills of software tools were higher than the cost of paying someone. I want someone who already has the tools and resources. I can leverage their investment, which saves me time. So, when people work with you, they pay you because of where they are. They work with you because of where they want to go—the promise!

You'll have more success in your conversations if you talk about where working with you will get them. If you can answer this proactively in your email and messaging, your conversations will be much more impactful.

Let's say you sell pain medication. People aren't going to reach out to you because they want to keep their headaches. They're going to buy from you because they don't want the headache. They want to be pain-free. That's the future outcome; this is the Promise.

Remember when we talked about the transformation? In other words, what will happen for the client by working with you? When it becomes clear to clients that you are the best step toward their promise, where they want to go, you will hear yes more often. You will end up with better clients who are happy to pay you, excited to work with you, and who tell other people about their experience.

I call the distance between where they are and where they're going the sales distance. So, the farther apart they are, the more they will pay. This contrast allows you to build value where there is no obvious pain.

The more urgent the need, the faster they will pay you. This is where the pain comes in. Let me not just dismiss the fact that there needs to be a reason for them to move. The mistake we often make is not being clear on why they want change and where they need your help. They're not hiring you because they want to stay in that position. They're hiring because they want to get to their future outcome. The promise closes the distance between where they are and where they want to go. That's where you come in and leverage better questions to create better clients.

We're going to ask questions about what they hope to achieve. Then ask, Why haven't you done that already? Why are you in your current position and not your future position?

By asking better questions, you make better decisions, which yields better results. The same holds true for those people you want as clients. They also need to ask better questions. You want to guide this process using the 4P Framework. That's how we grow revenue, improve retention, and build better businesses. It is simple but not always easy.

Where we're going is as important as the problem they have getting there. The promise is why they talk to us. The problem is why they buy from us. The disconnect between the two is what I call sales distance. It is the journey between where they are and where they want to go. It's how impactful and valuable your solution is to them.

You may not be able to take them all the way to where they want to go, but you need to be able to show that you can get them closer. The language you use in marketing materials, social media, and sales conversations will reflect where you want to go. It's going to reflect the promise, the desired future outcome.

Ignoring the promises prevents those sales conversations from ever happening. We often get stuck where they are and don't talk about where they're going.

I love mathematics. Let me share a quick, simple definition of a line. A line connects a set of points, and the simplest line has two points: A and B. That's important when we talk about the promise. I see this missing from how we currently approach sales. We often spend so much time concerned with the need or the pain that we miss the expected outcome.

Ignoring the sales distance can make or break a future client's decision to buy. By asking better questions, you can bridge the distance, giving the client a reason to work with you.

So, the question you should be asking to find better clients is: Where are they? And where do they want to go?

The next logical question is, where can we find them?

If I were to give someone a list or description of your "better client," would they be able to search and find them effectively? As I mentioned in the last section, your description needs to be so clear that just about anyone can identify that external customer who exactly fits what you are looking for. It also needs to be defined well so that you can deliberately and intentionally go after more of those people.

If they are not easy to locate, pause to ask yourself, how clearly do we understand who this person is? Again, maybe by asking a better question, you will get a better answer.

I was talking with a client who serves couples. They wanted to know where they could find couples. I encouraged them to ask a better question: What is the promise? In other words, where do they want to go?

The client used what they had learned from our interactions and thought deeper, looking at the question as the answer. When I asked again where the client wanted to go, they replied, "Reduced stress and sustaining long, healthy, happy marriages." Now that is the promise. That's where the better client wants to go. When you're clear on what that looks like, your language changes. It becomes clear who you are talking to and makes it easy to locate them. When you are clear on where they want to go, it becomes easier to talk to them. Better questions. Better clients.

Of course, this is just one example, and there are literally hundreds, if not thousands, of possible questions we could ask. That's why you will not find a list of questions in this book. I don't want to teach you what to think. I want to show you HOW to create your own questions, which become easier with practice.

Because we know what they're looking for and what they're spending their time on, we can meet them where they are and help them get to where they want to go. That's where the promise comes in and helps us find better clients. Figure out what they are typing into Google and work backward from there. Write down how you do this so you can repeat it. That should be part of your process.

PROCESS - HOW DO WE CREATE THE DESIRED RESULT CONSISTENTLY?

You want results. From your customer success team, marketing team, or sales team. This advice can apply to any department. It doesn't have to be about sales. It is why you picked up this book. Your focus is on revenue and retention. If we can create revenue, we can address all the other challenges in the business. When you find something that works, you may ask: How do we do it again? This process allows us to promise our clients results. With a clear process, we can answer the question: How can we duplicate success?

By now, you should be clear on who we serve with excellence. You should be able to articulate the promise clearly. Our next set of questions will answer HOW we will serve them—the process!

To duplicate success, you must have a repeatable process. How are we going to build successful partnerships? How can we confidently serve them with excellence over and over again? There should be a process for finding and serving them.

You don't just want customers one time. How do we foster loyalty? How do we turn our customers into referral partners? This is where our questions drive revenue. The search for the answer increases customer retention.

Let's talk about the process.

Internal

As we've talked about, there are two areas where we need to focus: internal and external clients. If you take care of your people, you take care of your business. The process section of the 4P Framework helps you document HOW we are going to do that. How do we help our team excel? Don't hire people and hope they figure it out. Succeed on purpose!

All too often, I've gone into an organization, and they say, "Here's your login." There really wasn't an onboarding process past my I-9 form. Instead, I had to figure out how to succeed. That was their strategy. Hire a bunch of people, and if you sold, you could stay. If not, you could leave or be terminated for underperformance. This isn't a scalable practice. You can reverse engineer a strong onboarding process by asking the inverse question. Why do people leave? No guesses. If you don't know the answer to the question, I have a suggestion for you: ask. Conduct exit interviews and check with HR about offering an incentive. I suggest something short and focused. Choose a few questions and one blank space for feedback. You should ask them to rate their response from 1-5. Do not give them essay prompts. Specific questions are going to help you the most. The blank space is for their ideas and suggestions you may not have thought to ask.

Take those answers and ask yourself: "What can we do on the front end to avoid this outcome?" What processes can we put in place to make the onboarding process simpler and ensure that we retain good people? When you know and understand why people leave your organization, you can create a process for them to thrive.

Here's the next question: What can we do that encourages the best people to grow and underperformers to leave? The answer to this question will help shape your culture and your training. This is going to help you create a company where your clients are excited to work with your team members. Again, this is where we generate revenue. Those are the people paying you. It's not just putting snacks in a break room or paying more. If you paid double the salary of similar roles, would there be room for profit growth? What if you paid 25% more salary than average and focused on marketing to a premium buyer? This question isn't a performative exercise. It's necessary in order to build.

This is the foundation and catalyst of your business growth. What questions do we need to ask in order to achieve better outcomes? That's where we are going. Once we have direction, we are on a path toward success. We can repeat this process for the customer success team. These questions aren't unique to sales teams, but I know that if you can increase revenue, you can figure out the rest of the business problems.

I also encourage you to ask this question in an interview. "Hey, why do you want to come work for us?" "There are 33 million businesses registered in the US. Why would you come to work for us?" This is not the why should we hire you question. That is a poor question, anyway. You are trying to learn how they perceive your company so you can do more of what is working. As you ask this question consistently, you will start to uncover your unique value. You can use the answer to attract better talent. "What makes your company special?" Most businesses are not unique. You're not the only company that manufactures cars or builds software.

Please don't let your ego stop you from receiving this lesson. There is someone who does something similar or exactly the same. How do you set yourself apart? I will give you a hint. Part of the answer to the question is WHY you built the business in the first place.

External

So now, if we are talking about external customers, the goal is not to build some magical product that no one's ever heard of. That isn't as much fun as it sounds. Before the consumer buys, a lot of education has to happen. How? By creating the processes for your sales representatives, customer-facing roles, etc. You need to teach them these concepts of asking better questions so they can identify with the external client, making the process faster, smoother, and more appealing.

Everyone internally should be able to articulate the promise and the reason their favorite clients chose them. This should be part of your processes. How are the answers communicated? Where are the answers stored? How often are their knowledge checks?

I do training on this called "Three Cs of compelling communication"—confident, concise, and clear. We use this framework when communicating the transformation. Again, this is a process. It ensures everyone uses very similar language and messaging. If you would like to learn how this simple and powerful training can help your team, email bruce@ newskillsnewyou.com with "3Cs" in the subject line.

If you cannot write down the steps, you have a problem. If the process is not clear, it's not repeatable. It's not going to be predictable, duplicatable, or scalable. Write it down!

Let me ask you: Can you consistently predict the team or company's success? If it's about business growth and strategy overall, what is your process to get you where you want to go?

On a higher level, everyone should understand the company's overall vision. These processes apply to every department. Any team can ask better questions and get better results. Anytime there is uncertainty, ask questions. Whenever there is a lack of clarity, ask questions. If it's not working, something is missing. Of course, it is tough to admit something's wrong. It may hurt your pride, but the questions you are not asking are costing you money.

There are four perspectives you should explore as you write out your process:

- How do we train the process to our PEOPLE?
- How do we communicate the PROMISE?
- How do we document the PROCESS?
- How does our PRICING support the above?

Let's explore an example where process or the lack of process impacts growth.

You picked this book up because you are looking for a strategy to increase revenue and improve retention. Imagine you get a spike of 100 customers.

One hundred new customers all in one day could be exciting. Is your team equipped to support them well? Now, fast-forward a year, and they all churn. Now, you need one hundred new customers. How would that impact morale? How would that impact revenue? Something exciting quickly turned into a huge concern.

To increase revenue, retain clients, and develop the business, you must focus on this three-part question: "How do we attract, keep, and grow clients for our business?"

The answer lies in your processes.

PRICING - HOW DOES THIS SUPPORT BUSINESS GROWTH AND MAKE SENSE TO THE CLIENT?

Now that the previous Ps have been addressed within the framework, people, promise, and process, it is only natural for a potential client to ask, "How much is it going to cost us to get there?"

In SaaS, there is a phrase, "up and to the right." When you are looking at an XY graph of your revenue, the line should trend upwards from left to right. This means your revenue is increasing. I call it going the right way. I truly believe that if you have consistent revenue growth in your business, you can take care of everything else. You don't have to beg for loan approvals, dance and jump through hoops for grants, or cater to investors. You can fund your own growth.

Everything is a lot easier when you have consistent revenue growth. In fact, all of those become optional when you have net profit to show. Is it the most important thing? That's up to you to decide. Is it the only thing? Of course not! But that's what we're focusing on. We are focusing on the questions we are not asking that are costing us money. If you create one question that brings you one additional client, this book will have a remarkable ROI for you.

Marketing, sales, and even customer success all impact company growth. Their roles and success in their roles are predicated by a strong pricing strategy. This topic could be an entire separate book.

In this chapter, we're going to talk about pricing questions. How do we choose the right price? What questions do we need to ask to make sure the price attracts the right client? How do we make sure the price is best for the business while still being attractive to the customer? Those are good questions, and to answer them, we need some context. We need to understand price versus value. Value is what they get, while price is what they pay. I did not invent this. How do we communicate our value so well that the price is not a barrier to a yes?

I was working with an entrepreneur, and I realized they were undercharging. This isn't about knowing your value—knowing your worth is a spiritual conversation. They were charging under what the market set. This isn't about telling you you're special. There's only one you; you are unique. That is all true, but we are talking about running a profitable business.

This client was selling below the market and offering above-average service for a far below-average price. It was costing them money to bring on new clients. This is a terrible long-term strategy. I wrote this for them because I realized that if I could teach them to increase their prices, I could help them increase their business on all levels.

The solution was simple. They asked past clients, "What is the service worth to you?" What would you be willing to pay? The clients saw value in their offering. Their responses were 2x to 10x greater than the current price. Then, we increased the price to match the average of their responses. The result was the same time, the same effort, the same number of clients, but a 5X increase in revenue.

Please don't miss the application because your business is XXX employees and you're not a solo entrepreneur. The lesson is simple. You don't decide the value; your client does. You articulate the value. This is where the promise meets a dollar amount. We communicate the promise in a confident, clear, and concise manner. You must communicate the price the same way. Easy to understand is easy to decide.

Pricing should be simple. I shouldn't have to take a math class to understand how your pricing works. Your pricing may vary, so give them a range. Your pricing shouldn't be a secret. If you don't want to post your pricing publicly, make it easy for the ideal customer to obtain. If people are serious about getting away from their problems and closer to the promise, they are not going to disappear when you say the price. Be bold and confident in your pricing.

A simple formula to remember is VALUE>PRICE>COST.

What if technology lowers cost? How do we justify the price and increase value? The cost of producing and delivering software will decrease. It is becoming much more accessible to build and deploy software, and pricing is going to be influenced by this evolution. Now, clients' expectations are changing. Hey, look, the cost is greater than the value. That's the wrong way. The better approach is keeping the value greater than the cost. That is a winning formula. The challenge becomes understanding what is valuable to the client or future client and then asking how we can deliver this most efficiently. For SaaS, I believe this is the level of service and support the client receives after purchase. CX teams are going to be infinitely valuable. Proactive support will be standard. And their skills are going to mirror coaches or consultants.

When we talked about the promise, we talked about the transformation and asking the question, where are they going to end up because they work with us? How much time, energy, and money is it going to take them to get there? That's the process. How do we get them there smoothly? The value is what they get, the price is what they pay, and the cost is running our business.

If the price is less than the cost, you're going backward. That's pretty easy. But we have to make sure our decisions are based on solid answers to our questions, not speculation or guessing. If you don't know the answer, test it. Your goal is to support business growth and have the client's best interest in mind. The client's success is your success, but not at the expense of the business. What is the customer's expectation? What do they want or need from us? Prioritize ease of use and simple adoption. It doesn't have to be both. If you have both, you have a winning idea.

Ease of use and simple adoption mean making it easy for them to do business with you and to get to the transformation. People will pay for that. Assume that there are two options of the same price; they will very likely choose the one that's easier.

I am providing this information as a framework, but I recommend you spend your time and energy on growing your business. One suggestion is to create a premium offer. What can you provide that is above the market? Doing this will put you in the premium category. The client who is looking for quality and excellence will be attracted to this, and they understand there's a higher cost associated with that. I will very rarely tell you to lower your prices.

Make your pricing simple and easy to understand. I want to make it easy for you to decide to work with me. That's really what I want everyone to get. A potential client should not be confused trying to figure out if your product or service is worth the value. We want them to say, "Let's figure out how to pay for it." You don't want to have to convince people to work with you.

This may be the most valuable question you ask: How do we make our pricing simple and easy to understand?

If you can do that, you take care of a lot of the other problems. You want to be able to articulate why you are charging the client this amount. The value should be higher than the price. Keep it simple.

You're on your way to getting better clients and growing your business.

_____

_____

_____

_____

_____

_____

_____

_____

_____

_____

_____

_____

_____

_____

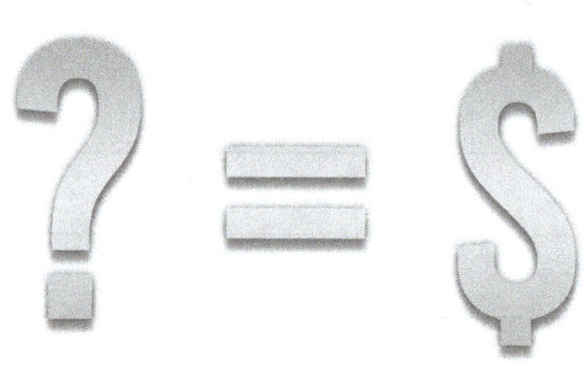

HOW DO YOU ANSWER: WHAT DO YOU DO?

New Skills New You, LLC was created on the principle that growing your people is also growing your business. **Learning one new skill will change your life!** And that new skill? Teaching your people how to ask better questions to gain better clients. I found within all the certifications and years of experience one obvious truth. **Simple wins.** I've explored many different industries, but at the end of the day, the most simple training is the most effective. That's what we're going to do in this book. We're going to keep this very simple. Some of this you might already know, but the true value is in executing what you know and learn. Ultimately, making sure you are doing the right thing in the right order at the right time.

Let's begin with a familiar question. When someone asks, "What do you do?" How do you answer?

When speaking to potential clients, there are actually four questions that you should keep in mind and develop responses for each to best answer this question.

Let's look at your own company or team; then, we can use this to help you ask your potential and future clients the right questions. Sometimes, the quality of our answers is limited or improved by the quality of our questions.

1. Who are you?
2. Why do you do what you do?
3. What is the transformation you provide?
4. How do you do what you do?

Let's break these down.

Who are you? While many of us start out by answering this quickly and easily when asked, it is actually the least important answer to the overall goal of converting a potential client into a paying client. You don't care whether my name is Bruce or that I was born in Ohio. There may be some connection to the person you are speaking to, but more than likely, it will not help you achieve a conversion.

I am always careful with the commonly used phrase "know, like, and trust." I think it's both informative and inaccurate. Clients have to know you to work with you because they can't work with someone they've never met. But they don't need to like you to work with you. It's not a popularity contest. If their acceptance of you is a requirement, then your mom would be your best client. But your mom is very likely not your ideal client. So, I don't recommend you spend your energy on being likable. Be yourself!

However, I will concede this small point: if there are two options of equal prices, the client will choose the person they like the most. But we can't let popularity be the only reason people work with us. That's not a sustainable business model. A client's likeness of you is valuable but misses the point.

You may be thinking, "Well, Bruce, what about trust?" I believe people decide to trust you once you prove it. You have to make it easy for them to trust you. In reality, they can't really trust you because they haven't worked with you before. Yes, credibility is proof of concepts. This could be a referral or testimonial from a past client. But inevitably, they have to choose to trust first, and then work can be done to build (and maintain) that trust. Trust must be present for them to refer you to others. When a client decides to work with you, they are agreeing to do so without knowing what the outcome will be.

Sales is a transfer of enthusiasm, belief, and confidence. If I'm confident you can and will do what you say, I will decide to trust you. Now, you have a customer who is excited to work with you because you proved them right. Their enthusiasm will encourage them to tell others to work with you, too! So, as you can see, to answer the question of 'who are you?' it is more appropriate to respond in a way that will establish trust over popularity or even minor details such as your background or upbringing.

Why do you do what you do? As Simon Sinek says in his book *Start With Why*, when speaking with a client for the first time, you have the opportunity to connect emotionally with them and show them why your work matters—not just to you, but to them as well. If you have not read Sinek's book or watched his Ted Talk "How Great Leaders Inspire Action," I highly recommend doing so, especially if you are a leader, speaker, coach, or entrepreneur. You will find these resources, along with others, at the back of the book to help you grow and develop personally and professionally. The answer to the question, Why do you do what you do, lays the foundation for the passion, values, and impact behind your actions.

What is the transformation you provide? The real question the client may be thinking is, what happens because I work with you? What happens after I pay you?? Ninety days from now, what does my life or business look like? Many people likely provide the same or similar products or services. How do you offer something transformational to the client that the others may not? There are very few industries that truly do something no one else does. Even if that's true for the moment, their methods will be copied very quickly. This is a very important metric to have an answer to. To answer this question, you must identify and communicate the real, meaningful change that your product or service delivers to your customers. It's not just about the features or benefits—it's about the before and after impact on their life or business. Revisit the chapter on PROMISE.

For example:

A fitness coach doesn't just offer workouts—they help clients gain confidence, energy, and a healthier lifestyle.

A marketing consultant doesn't just provide strategies—they help businesses grow revenue, attract ideal clients, and build a strong brand.

A home cleaning service doesn't just clean houses—it creates a stress-free, comfortable living environment for families.

By focusing on transformation, you show potential customers the real value of what you offer and why they should choose you over competitors.

How do you do it? This is where most people usually get stuck. The problem is that they start here. Don't be most people. Until the client decides they want this transformation, how you give them the transformation becomes irrelevant. The question of "how?" is for after they say, "Yes, we're interested" or "Okay, let's do this." Only then is it time to talk about implementation.

Now that the client has decided to proceed with the transformation, we can discuss the "how" of the process. As an example, let's use my business. There are workshops, live training, digital courses, and books. That is how my business teaches clients to increase their revenue. That's the transformation. Why? I believe that one new skill will change your life. I believe that growth within your people is the best way to grow your business.

So, if you are now wondering how these four questions will help you grow personally and professionally, I have already got you thinking the right way—you are already thinking about better questions.

Think of the reason you picked up this book. You saw that the goal was driving revenue and improving retention through personal and professional development. If I can help you turn more conversations with the clients into business, that is a good investment of your money. If I can help you hear YES more often, that is a good investment of your time. Well, good news. You are headed in the right direction. Investing in your people allows your business to grow faster and more smoothly, approve retention, and turnover increase profit. Investing in your people is investing in your business. That being said, this book is not just about asking questions, but rather, it is about how you invest in your people, teaching them how to ask better questions to attract better clients.

Ultimately, I wrote this for you—**the people leaders, business owners, and entrepreneurs**. In our fast-paced, highly technical world, I am finding that people, both our internal customers (aka employees) and external customers (aka clients), are often overlooked. We start following popular trends instead of asking questions that guide better decisions. The questions you are not asking are costing you money. When I hear the same thing over and over again, that often signals to me that there is a problem. If I see a problem enough times, I take note. I have heard all too often people, leaders, business owners, and entrepreneurs say that they struggle to find the right client or the client "almost" purchased or maybe even the employee was not meeting their quota. I saw a problem, and based on my own personal experiences, I was determined to find a solution.

As I shared at the beginning of the book, I discovered that when I started asking better questions, I became more clear in my decision-making, sales approach, and, ultimately, revenue growth.

This book was born because I spent money on software that was a waste of time and on training and courses that didn't provide an ROI.

I aim to help you avoid repeating this mistake. Before you invest in a trainer, buy expensive software, integrate artificial intelligence, or fill in the blank, you must learn what questions you need to ask. How can I create a framework to educate others? How can we create a system that can be used over and over again? One that can be implemented and iterated quickly and works for the largest number of people with the greatest positive impact?

By asking myself and others many questions, I came up with the 4P framework (People, Promise, Process, and Price), which includes the questions you need to change and the answers you find. You've probably asked yourself many of these questions before, but you haven't asked them intentionally. My goal is to use what you already know and put it in a useful framework—that is where clarity and results happen.

I will give you one simple idea and encourage you to use it in all of your interactions with your teams and employees, potential clients, and even in your personal life: **Asking better questions gets better answers.**

I will credit my friend Bill McCleskey of Mitech Partners with saying, "The question is the answer."

Of course, no matter your role, position, company, or status, we have all asked the question, how can we grow faster? What is the best way to use this investment? Why can't we make any money? Why are we talking to so many people, and only some of them say yes? Unfortunately, in many cases, this is where it stops. But if you are bold enough to say, "That was a good question—let's find the answer," I guarantee that you will open the door to new opportunities, growth, revenue, and potential.

I aim to help you create a strategy that consistently and predictably leads to healthy growth and improves your customer retention. Now, if you are in business, you know that doesn't happen by accident. Success happens on purpose by asking better questions.

Inside the Better Questions Toolkit there is a section on crafting a strong introduction

Scan the QR Code use code Book

HOW DO WE DEFINE BETTER CLIENTS?

So, I have mentioned several times already that we are looking for better clients. But what is a better client? A better question may be, Whom can we serve the best with our product or service? No matter the industry, product, or service, everyone is looking for that ideal customer or client that pays on time, appreciates your work, and is easy to work with. Now, while this sounds great, what are we really talking about? The phrase "better clients" generally refers to customers who are more aligned with your business values, are easier to work with, and contribute to long-term success.

Better yet, who can we serve with excellence? There are many people you can work with, but there are a few people you can serve with excellence. We want to find those people. First, we must identify them, and then we can find them.

The definition of "better client" can vary depending on your goals, but here are some common characteristics of better clients:

- Higher Value – They are willing to pay for quality and see the value in your work.
- Respectful & Professional – They treat you and your team with respect and appreciate your expertise.
- Clear Communicators – They articulate their needs and expectations well, making collaboration smoother.
- Loyal & Long-Term – They return for repeat business, refer others, and build lasting relationships.
- Aligned with Your Niche – They fit your ideal customer profile, meaning you can deliver exceptional results with ease.
- Timely & Reliable – They pay on time, meet deadlines, and honor agreements.

Essentially, better clients make your work more fulfilling, profitable, and sustainable while reducing stress and unnecessary challenges. This is where we'll start seeing improvement in your growth—seeing better clients, not just more clients.

Isn't this what every business owner or company wants and strives for? Isn't this what all businesses build their marketing strategies around? The way I see it, it is actually very simple: ask better questions—get better clients!

Of course, having more clients is good, and from a ratios perspective, the more clients you have, the more likely you are to have better clients. But what if you could have better clients AND achieve all of your sales goals without having to increase the number of clients or break the bank with your marketing and/or advertising budget?

Again, I will remind you of the basic concept I want to share: ask better questions and get better answers/clients!

So, from a practical perspective, what constitutes a better client? The best clients don't need convincing. If you have to persuade people to work with you, it means one of two things: they are either the wrong client or they lack confidence in your ability to deliver a solution. Better clients pay on time. Better clients value what you do. They respect you as an individual and as a business. They refer you to others. Great clients leave outstanding reviews. Better clients practice strong communication. They come back and want to work with you again.

On the other hand, what type of client might you be getting currently? A bad client? Ones that only present you with more problems, issues, and headaches? I don't want you just to have more clients if that means more headaches. That could mean more people that you have to fight with to get on board. It could mean more late payments, fewer referrals, and less reviews, or worse, a bad review. They could be unresponsive or respond with poor communication.

Frankly, you don't just want more clients—you want fewer bad ones and many more good ones!

So, let's be very intentional when we say better clients. These are the types of clients who help your business grow. My goal is to help you ensure you attract and win clients with whom you want to work and who want to work with you.

As a business owner and coach, that's my mission— to help you identify what defines "better clients" in your industry or market. How do you identify them? What do they look like?

I do not want to set the expectation that I will be providing you with a list of questions to ask or give you the exact way of defining better clients for your specific industry. No! There are just too many unique situations, markets, and clients to do this. What I will provide throughout the next chapters are thought-provoking ideas and concepts that will help you develop and ask the questions most appropriate for your industry or situation. I will teach you to find and define the questions yourself to match your unique business environment. If you need help clarifying your client avatar, email **bruce@newskillsnewyou.com** and put "better clients" in the subject line.

_____

_____

_____

_____

_____

_____

_____

_____

_____

_____

_____

_____

_____

_____

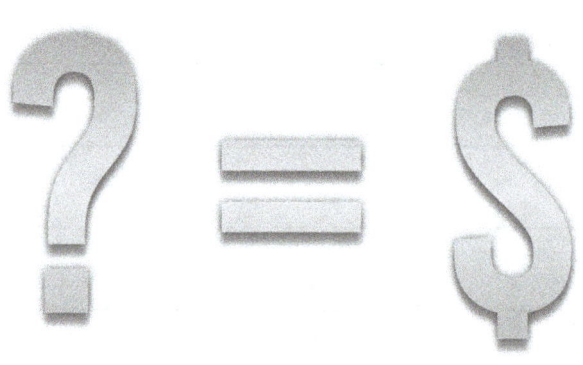

HOW DO WE ASK BETTER QUESTIONS

We all use questions in our daily conversations. But are they always a productive or efficient use of our time? Do they sometimes require follow-up or leave you wanting more information? This chapter will discuss how to use questions more effectively. When you use questions well, it expands the depth of your conversation. It opens up new ideas and explores possibilities. It also helps to reach a decision faster. Remember, great questions get great answers.

As I mentioned earlier, "The question is the answer." Sales is often more about teaching, but that starts with engaging clients. You cannot teach someone if they are not willing to learn. Sales is not something you do for or to someone. Just like learning, you cannot force someone to do an action. You cannot SELL someone something against their will or self-interest. You can only hope to facilitate the buying decision.

My conclusion is simple. Sales is an educational process. Questions are the guides along the way. So, how do you know what they know or their willingness to even learn more without asking the right questions?

I love to hear clients say, "Hmm, I never thought of it that way."

It is incredibly rewarding for them to exclaim, "Yes! I get it now!"

Questions help engage the client in their learning journey.

I wanted to write a business development book, not pure sales training, with an emphasis on strategy and planning. What better way to strategize and plan than to begin with the basics—understanding what questions to ask to engage clients.

When I started out, I also knew that I wanted to keep it simple. So, let's start with the foundation of this entire premise. What does it mean to ask better questions?

Let's set some definitions: question

/ˈkwesCH(ə)n/

noun

plural noun: questions

a sentence worded or expressed as to elicit information.: synonyms: inquiry, query, interrogation, examination, quiz, quizzing

antonyms: answer, response

There are two fundamental types of questions: **open-ended questions and closed-ended questions**.

I taught this to a group of mental health professionals, many of whom were therapists. They were really good at using questions to get clients to open up or think outside the box. I taught them how to apply those same questioning skills to their business. Yes, it's a skill—one that you will find to be life-changing when learned and implemented!

Open-ended questions should be used to gather information. The goal is to gain insights into the client. These questions generally cannot be answered with a simple yes or no but rather require an additional response, stimulating an actual conversation. Remember, better questions = better clients.

Open-ended questions will usually begin with an adverb such as who, what, where, when, why, and how. This will take some practice since many of us are accustomed to asking simple questions that often can be answered with a yes or no. Unfortunately, this approach to gathering information can very quickly sound like an interview. Or worse, it can feel like an invasive interrogation. However, I don't want you to overcomplicate the process. Questions are a very natural part of any conversation, and when asked in a way that requires additional input, you also build trust and relationships.

The other type of question is a closed-ended question. These can be answered with a simple yes or no and generally start with a verb.

For example:

- Do you want to move forward?
- Are you hungry?
- Did you have a good day at school?
- Will you buy my product?

Have you ever been on a date and the conversation was just dry? You're sitting there trying not to stare into space. Your eyes are dry because you are bored. Boring questions = boring conversation.

- Did you have a good day? ~ Yes
- Did you have a hard time finding the place? ~ No
- Do you know what you want to eat? *YAWN* ~ Yes

What if you changed the approach slightly and asked the same questions, just a little differently?

- What was the most interesting part of your day?
- What do you know about this restaurant?
- What are some of your favorite foods?

See the difference between the two? Better questions = better conversations. Yes, these are safe, first-date questions. If you are bold, ask some bold questions. Good luck on your second date!

Let's turn my original examples into open-ended questions to see how we can spark the conversation and gather better information.

- What are your hesitations about moving forward?
- How hungry are you?
- What did you learn in school today?
- How many [product(s)] do you want?

When you change your tactic, using open-ended questions instead of those requiring only a one-word response, you will see the depth and breadth of your conversation expand. Close-ended questions are not "bad questions," but they should be used sparingly, less than 20% of the time, or in a 5:1 ratio. They are best used for confirmation. In a business setting, I use closed-ended questions to make sure the client and I are on the same page. I most often use them towards the end of the call once I have a clear understanding of the problem, challenges, goals, and vision.

HOW TO USE QUESTIONS IN A CONVERSATION

My recommendation is to use more open-ended questions than closed-ended questions. More open-ended questions create better conversations. Better conversations turn into better clients.

Here is a sample conversation of how you might use open-ended questions at the beginning of a call:

YOU: Hi, I'm Bruce. Before we get started, tell me how to pronounce your name.

CLIENT: [NAME]

YOU: Wonderful [NAME]. Thank you for being punctual; we appreciate you a lot!

CLIENT: No problem! I'm excited to talk with you today.

YOU: Most people schedule this call because they want to invest in themselves and/or their people with the aim of having an even more successful business. Is that true for you?

CLIENT: Yes, exactly.

YOU: Okay, great! You're in the right place. Most of these conversations take 30-40 minutes, depending on the number of questions you have. Is this still a good time for you?

CLIENT: I have a hard stop at HH: MM.

YOU: Okay! That gives us plenty of time. To help you find the best solution for you, may I ask a few questions?

CLIENT: Sure, what do you want to know?

YOU: Tell me how you have invested in your people in the past and what you would do differently this time.

Let's look at this process of asking better questions from another perspective.

Imagine you are driving to your friend's house. Your friend lives far out in the country, in a beautiful, wooded area. Unfortunately, there is very little cellular reception, and you get lost.

What do you do?

As you are riding in the car, you go slowly, reading every sign and checking your cell phone for signals. Praying to the wireless gods for just a few bars of signal and a few kilobytes of data. Eventually, you see a small convenience store. You pull into the parking lot and go inside.

The clerk greets you warmly, and you ask them for help. Without thought, the clerk will ask you a few questions.

- Who is your friend?
- What is your friend's address?
- Do you know what the house looks like?
- Do you have their number?

You give them the address, but it is a new property that isn't on any physical map yet. The clerk hands you a landline phone and allows you to call your friend. Your friend answers and asks a question: "Who is this?" "Oh, hey." "Where are you?" "Okay, great, you're really close."

You type the directions into your phone, thank the clerk for their help, and return to your car. You make it to your friend's house without any other issues, and you both have a warm reunion.

What if the convenience store was closed? Maybe the clerk was rude. Imagine they gave you directions without even asking for the address, just random lefts and rights. How would that change the experience? How would the outcome of the story change?

Your client is the driver. The friend in this story is their desired outcome. You are the store clerk. You are their support and guide. You use questions to understand how to serve your client best. Questions help you discover exactly what they need.

The client is elated. They return, tell their friends good things about you, and think you are a genius.

I encourage you to keep asking questions until 1 of 3 things happens.

1. The client makes a decision (hopefully a yes buying decision)
2. The client starts asking you questions
3. They resist answering questions

If at any point the client says, "I'm ready to get started," stop asking questions and collect their payment information. Yes, that will happen. Don't talk yourself or the client out of a sale. This is your chance to change their life/business and help you grow your revenue. Take it!

This happens infrequently, but it does happen. The client comes on the call, ready to begin. Embrace those moments! The rest of the time, you will have to prompt for a decision.

Sometimes, the client will begin to ask you questions. Before diving into a lengthy and detailed explanation, respond to the question with another question.

"That is a good question [NAME]. Before I answer, what prompted you to ask this?" Be careful you don't sound defensive. "Why do you want to know that?!" can be accusatory, even hostile. When asked with compassion and curiosity, this question will help you understand WHY the client asked you this question. Here is a sample conversation:

CLIENT: How much does it cost?

YOU: Great question. I am happy to explore our pricing. Before we do tell, is cost your highest priority?

CLIENT: No, but our budget is kinda tight.

YOU: Do you have a separate budget for [your product or service]?

CLIENT: No, but this is something we have been talking about for a while.

YOU: How long is a while?

CLIENT: Oh, about 2-3 years now.

YOU: Sounds like this is a nice to have, not a need to have, is that correct?

CLIENT: Well, it is starting to be a bigger and bigger problem.

YOU: Well, I'm here to help. Do you mind if I ask a few more questions to recommend the best solution and price for you?

CLIENT: ...Yes, but I would really like a price before we continue; I don't want to waste any time.

YOU: Yes, of course. Our services range from $ to $$$$$. If we can find a solution for you and stay within that range, does it make sense to continue?

CLIENT: Okay, great. We need to be close to the $$ range that could work.

YOU: Wonderful. I have some amazing success stories from clients who chose options in that range. My goal is to help you do the same. Tell me more about...

Remember, if they are taking time out of their day to talk to you, they are already interested! A question is a good thing. When a client starts asking questions, you should be excited. This is an indication that they are open to your solution. Don't perceive questions as hostility or resistance.

Answer their questions briefly and with transparency. Keep control of the conversation.

PROTIP: Answer their question directly and end your response with another question.

Now, sometimes, the client gets annoyed by questions. They may say, "I don't want to answer these questions; I just need the price" (refer to the conversation example).

They refuse to answer questions. They could try to rush you and say they are in a hurry. Have any of these happened to you?

Keep your composure and excuse yourself from the conversation. Yes, it is good for you to tell the client no. Choosing to deny working with someone may be the toughest part of the job. It feels like you are saying no to the money. Trust me, it is good for your business and great for your peace. This may be more difficult than asking for the money. Saying no is counterintuitive, but it is important.

Use this phrase whenever you get an unpleasant person on the call.

"Sounds like I caught you at a bad time. Please reschedule as soon as you can. I look forward to hearing from you."

This is not a question. This is not a suggestion. My business is helping people, not convincing people to work with me. If you want to argue, join a debate team.

For people leaders, business owners, and entrepreneurs, better questions mean better clients.

I want to switch gears for a moment and discuss how questions can improve our business, not just help us land a new or "better" client.

When analyzing our business, revenue stream, or strategies, we often look at the negative. What's wrong or what's not working? But if you spend more time asking what is working and doing more of that, you will have a positive outlook. By default, spend less time doing things that aren't working. This goes back to my previous statement, "The question is the answer."

- What are we doing well?
- What do we need to do less of?
- What do we need to do more of?
- What do we need to start doing?

In other words, how can you maximize what you already do well? Whether you are looking to gain better clients, increase your revenue, or reduce your costs, it all begins with Asking Better Questions.

Asking better questions is more than a thought exercise. The end result is better clients. However, it doesn't work unless you do the work. This, of course, leads me to the strategy I use for asking better questions in several key areas, which we will get into in the next chapter.

_____

_____

_____

_____

_____

_____

_____

_____

_____

_____

_____

_____

_____

_____

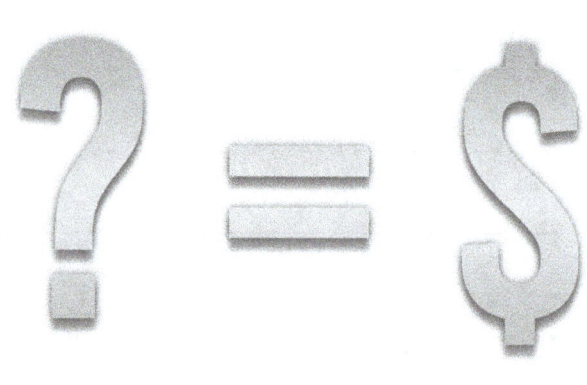

BONUS

Authors Note

This was added after the final edit. But I thought it was important to share. Please forgive any grammatical errors

I discovered a new way to evaluate the quality and effectiveness of our questions. I call it the goal of the question. There are two purposes or reasons to ask a question. You want to gain CONTEXT for understanding or learn some CONCRETE information.

Context questions explore "why" These questions will help you understand their thought process. Use them to explore how they make decisions. Learn about their motivation.

Concrete questions are used for specific data. There is usually only one answer to these questions. Think of a job/credit application or client intake form.

Neither of these is better than the other. They should be used intentionally depending on your goal.

Choose two highlighter colors. I like blue and yellow. As you read the rest of this book Highlight which ones are context questions and which ones are concrete questions. You can have you team do the same as you create questions for your business.

Be aware each of these can be both closed-ended or open-ended questions.

Because this may be a new concept for you. Check out the YouTube channel for a deeper dive on asking better questions

_____

_____

_____

_____

_____

_____

_____

_____

_____

_____

_____

_____

_____

_____

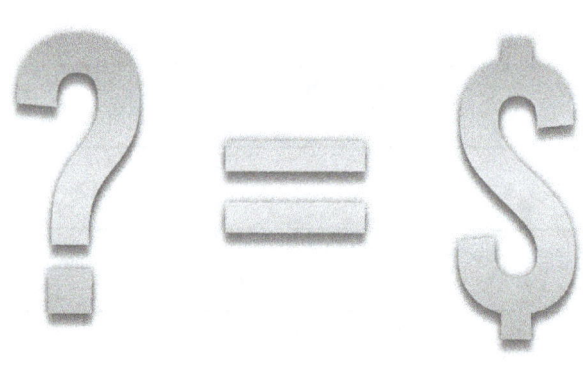

TURNING CONVERSATIONS INTO CLIENTS

Iused to call this the question path. It was a framework to help even the shyest introvert guide their client from interest to invoice. It was a simple step-by-step path anyone could follow. No magic script will convince 100% of the people to say yes. If someone tries to sell you such a thing, ask them for some magic beans, too. Instead, I want to create the greatest likelihood that the right client will tell you YES.

I have created this easy five-step process to follow. Let's get started.

1. Ask for permission

I like to start my calls with gratitude. It puts the potential client at ease and brings positive energy to the call, moving them to a positive frame of mind. You can start with a quick check-in. Do not ask, "How is your day going?" This is a poor question. It can feel a bit forced or even insincere and can quickly devolve into a rambling account of everything that happened to them that day. Now, you have spent 30 minutes without accomplishing anything.

A better question is: What prompted you to schedule a call today? I would also ask, "What do we need to cover for this call to be a success?" These are very focused questions. They get the client talking, and they have the added benefit of allowing you to double-check if this is the right person to be a client in your business.

For example, if someone calls me asking about their Section 8 voucher or food stamps, I know this is the wrong person for my business, and I save a lot of time. Think about your ideal client. What are one or two questions you can ask them to make sure they are the right person? For example, one of my clients is a publisher. He should ask every client, "Have you written a book?" The answer to this question determines the direction of the rest of the conversation.

2. Current situation

Once you are confident this is someone you are able to help, you need to understand their current situation. You are their guide, and in order to give them the best directions, you have to know where they are now. Even before you discuss their destination, your GPS does the same thing and often defaults to your current location. It happens automatically, so we often don't notice. The next time you use Google Maps, notice that there are always two points. Where you are going and where you are. You will give the client bad advice if you don't understand their current situation.

Years ago, a young man came into the car dealership. I showed him cool sports cars. They were bright colors, had two doors, and big engines—just fun cars to own and drive. But he didn't seem too excited. I started to ask about his current situation and why he was looking for a vehicle. I discovered he was expecting his first child, a little girl. Can you imagine me selling him a two-seater when he needs to have space for a child seat? I showed him small SUVs with space for a few adults and a car seat, and a good fit for a tight budget. He drove it home that day. He would have left frustrated if I hadn't understood where he was currently at in life and I would have been annoyed that he wasted my time. Not realizing I lost the sale because I didn't ask the right questions. Don't let that be you! Follow this framework and watch how you hear yes more often.

3. Future aspirations

Once you know where they are, find out where they want to go. Ask them about their dreams, goals, and aspirations. Ask them to paint a picture of what success looks like. If everything worked out better than you expected, what would life be like? What does success mean to you? If money was no longer a concern, what would you do more of? What would you do less of? It is imperative that you understand their hopes. Listen closely to the words they use. Is it clear and vivid? Or is it vague and poorly defined? The clearer the target, the better. You are going to reference this in your last stage when we present the solution. You can not give good directions if you don't know where they are going. You may tell them to drive 75 north when they want to go to Miami. The directions are good if you want to go to Canada, but they aren't the right directions for the client.

How do I know where the client wants to go? I ask them, "Why is this important?" The farther they are from their destination, the more they are willing to pay you to help them get there. People buy the transformation. You need to understand how far they want to go. The better you understand their future aspirations, the easier it will be to help them get there.

4. Frustration

DO NOT SKIP THIS STEP. If how far they will go determines how much they will pay you, then how frustrated they are will determine how quickly they will pay you. Let's say it is January. If I am getting married a year from now, I probably won't buy a tuxedo from you today. What if it is October or November, and I am getting married on New Year's Eve? I need to lose some weight to fit into my wedding dress. I will likely sign up right away for your fitness program. Ask questions here to find out how badly they want it. When they have a clear picture of their future aspirations, ask them what is in the way. What is stopping you from achieving that dream? Why haven't you done XYZ already? What is holding you back from the life you desire? The bigger the obstacle, the better you can be the hero. People will quickly pay when they are sick and tired of being sick and tired. They will pay when they feel lost and don't know what to do next. They will pay when they need results quickly. You don't have to convince people to work with you. You only need to show the right people why you are the best person to help them get from A to B. I like to ask the question, "What have you tried already?" Educate them on how you help them overcome their obstacles, and they will beg to pay you.

5. Present Solution

Now, it is time for you to do a little talking. If you use this framework, you should only be talking about 20% of the time. This is the end of the conversation and where your part begins. If you are an introvert and that is still too much talking for you, I would be happy to help you create a standard operating procedure so you can delegate this task.

I start by thanking them for sharing. "Bruce, thank you very much for giving me a peek into your world. I have helped clients in similar situations and would like to do the same for you. Can I share with you a little bit about our solution?"

Take some time to educate the customer on what you do and the result it will give them. Do not go into detail on HOW you solve their problems. This can be tedious and unnecessary. Most often, people want to know if you can give them the result they want. They just want to know if the desired transformation is possible for them! If anyone asks for more details, please share. I am not asking you to keep it a secret; be transparent. On the flip side, be careful you don't end up trying to teach them the whole 8-week program in less than an hour's conversation. This is counterproductive.

I like to give a testimonial here. Share with them a personal success story. Make sure to emphasize the points that most closely match the client's own experience. If you have them share a client testimonial, too, it can do wonders to show them what is possible. If you have a client with a similar background or matching demographics, use this to help them see that the cost yields results that can and will work for them.

I don't believe people have to know, like, or trust you to work with you. They have to have confidence that your solution will work for them. Trust is a choice. As long as you don't give them a reason NOT to trust you, they can decide to work with you. They have to trust you to refer you to friends or family. As they work with you, they will start to like you(because you're awesome!). Once they get the promised outcome, their decision to trust you will be proven. Now you have a lifelong advocate and customer!

PUT THE 4P FRAMEWORK TO USE

Now that you are familiar with the framework and we have covered the tools you need to leverage it, let's put it to use. This chapter will help you ask questions about yourself and your business. At the end of the chapter, there is space for you to write your own questions. I would love to hear your results. Share with me on linkedin or email Bruce@ newskillsnewoyu.com subject line Better Questions.

Warning: This may be the most mentally challenging activity in this book. Reach out to a friend or contact our team for help. Before we plan what questions to ask the customer or explore what question the customer is asking themselves, it is essential to ask yourself some key questions.

Consider this chapter an internal audit.

internal audit

noun

1

: a usually continuous examination and verification of books of account conducted by employees of a business—contrasted with an independent audit

2

: a review of systems of internal check and internal control of a business

If you manage a team, I encourage you to choose a few of these questions, let the team answer them, and compile them. How close are the team's answers to each other? How closely do they reflect the company's vision and standards? This exercise will help you identify blind spots in the team's understanding.

Sometimes, as individual coaches, speakers, and consultants, we make too many assumptions about why people pay us. It is negatively impacting your impact and your income. Do not skip this exercise. If you need some help, gift a copy of the book to a friend or mentor. Have them walk through the exercise with you. Grab another copy at www.askingbetterquestions. com.

- Who do I serve?
- Who picked this audience?
- Why did they pick this audience?
- Who is my ideal client?
- Whom can you serve with excellence?
- Where do I find my clients?
- Can I describe my ideal client well enough for someone else to find them?

- Who should I not work with?
- What problem do I solve?
- What solution(s) do I offer to solve these problems?
- Where do clients find me?
- How can I make it easy for clients to work with me?
- What do you say when people ask, "What do you do?"
- What is your most profitable offer?
- You can only offer one service/product for the year. What would you choose and why?
- What topic can you talk about for an hour without preparation?
- What was your easiest sale? How can you duplicate it?
- What do you love most about what you do?
- What do you like the least about what you do?
- Your client wants to work with you again. What will you offer them?

Pause and take a deep breath.

Did you just read the questions and keep going?

Did you pause and reflect?

Maybe you wrote down a few thoughts.

These questions are simple by design. If you take the time to give an honest answer, you will achieve a new depth of clarity.

When who you are and what you do are easy to understand, some very special things happen. First, you spend less time chasing poor-fit clients. Then, you waste less time convincing people to work with you and spend more time working with clients you enjoy doing what you love.

This is the power of questions. Better questions create better clients.

Here are a few questions many of my clients have difficulty answering.

What problem do you solve?

A marketing agent sent me a message asking if I wanted help.

I asked her, "What problem do you solve?"

She sent me the following message.

Social Media Content Funnel

DFY Appointment Setting

Inbox Management

Social media management

Scripting

Editing

She said, "Basically, do everything for you."

Notice something about her response? Most people do this. They confuse problems and solutions. Or worse, they ignore the PROMISE completely. They assume that if I tell you these amazing solutions I offer, you will automatically connect them to a problem you have and want to solve. This only works if I am aware of the problem I have AND what the possible solutions may be. If I were looking for a social media content funnel, this message would be right on time, but I'm not. Actually, I'm not sure what that is.

The problem with solutions is that the client often needs education. You're the expert, not them.

The client may not understand why or how your solution works for them. A few will get it immediately; however, you are missing a large percentage of potential clients.

Do you know what requires less education? PROBLEMS. If she said, "Stop wasting your time on social media; it's not making money. Schedule a call." I don't even know what solution she is offering, but I know I hate spending time on social media to make zero dollars. I would probably schedule the call.

The other question I see people struggle to answer is...

Who is your ideal client?

Who is a good referral for you?

They will say, everybody. But you don't speak any other language than English. How would you help someone who speaks Urdu or Q'eqchi'? How about German or Arabic? The point is that everyone isn't a real answer.

Okay, you say I help service-based businesses.

Plumbers?

Electricians?

Bricklayers?

No, not those types. Like software or IT companies.

How do you help them? I help them establish sales processes and business strategies.

I helped SaaS startups with less than 50 employees who have passed the first round of funding, seeking to create a formal sales process to facilitate revenue growth and reduce sales friction.

See the difference? I can find that person and introduce you. I can recognize them when I speak to them. I know exactly whom I should send to you as a referral.

Go back and review the questions again. Are your answers clear, concise, and compelling? Are your answers easy to understand? Explain it to a 9-year-old or a 90-year-old. Assume the person asking these questions has never heard of you or your industry.

Use the space provided to take notes. This is a workbook to help you grow your business. BONUS: These answers can be used in marketing materials or as part of onboarding for new hires.

_____

_____

_____

_____

_____

_____

_____

_____

_____

_____

_____

_____

_____

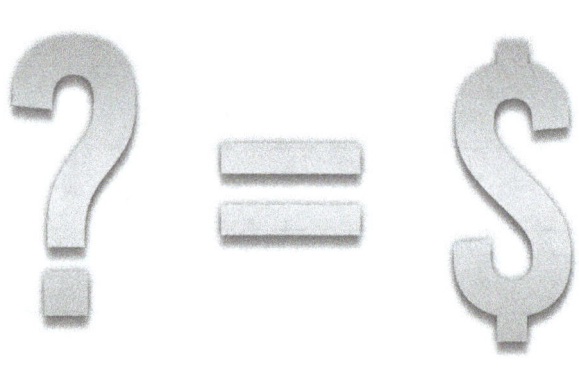

CASE STUDIES

It was very important to me that as you read this book, you also apply the information it provides. I try to use stories and real-world examples. I didn't want just to tell you what to do or even stop at how to do it. I hope I've done a good job at both. I want to show you why it's valuable. As I have said, sales is a transfer of enthusiasm, confidence, and belief. I want you to be excited about the possibilities this book creates for you. I hope that you are confident that this will work if you use it, and I want you to believe in yourself that the difference between here and your next level of success is the questions you ask.

Here are some case studies to show you other ways you can apply it to your life or business.

Customer Success Team

I know a customer success role involves 8+ positions all in one: customer service, leader, trainer, project manager, and so much more!

Part of writing this book involved interviewing customer success leaders across several different industries. Their insight has been a valuable part of making this book successful. You can see a list of these amazing individuals in the Special Thanks section!

You may ask, "Why is there a chapter on CSM teams in a sales book?" Here are two gentle reminders: Customer success is sales success. Also, this isn't a sales book. It is a strategy book on creating clarity that drives revenue and improves retention.

Let's use the 4P Framework from the lens of a Customer Success Leader.

PEOPLE. We have two internal clients: our fellow CSMs and the sales team. Coordinating with the sales team should be part of serving our external team with excellence. Only 8% mentioned training that collaborates directly with the sales team. Something to think about.

How well are the customers we are receiving fit to our definition of "better clients"?

How are we providing feedback to the sales team on customer status—good, bad, and ugly?

The answer to this question should be documented under "PROCESS."

When it is time to grow or renew an account, who is responsible? Does it go back to the sales team, an account manager or stay with the customer success team?

What metrics are we tracking to measure the quality of our service? Are we achieving the PROMISE we made to our clients?

Response time is an obvious metric. What about how often you reach out to the quiet customer? How are we tracking our team's success? How are they investing in their success? Not just product training but personal and professional development as well.

Where can we continually improve our customer experience?

One director said he spent a week recording answers to frequently asked questions, including tips on using their platform more effectively. He then gave the clients access to this knowledge library. In less than two years, the on-demand videos have accumulated 800+ hours! How are you saving your team time while creating flexibility for your customers?

What is our retention rate? What is our growth rate? Is our pricing simple to understand? Do customers call every month for an explanation of their invoice? Does our pricing support the company's profitability without driving away the customers we need to grow?

Perhaps you have answers to most of these questions. Maybe there are a few you need to reflect on.

EXERCISE: Ask your team members a few of these questions (I recommend 5-10) and see how many of them provide the same answers. The common answers affirm that everyone is on the same page. The outliers are signals of opportunity!

StartUp Founder

This is near and dear to me because this is where I started. The design of the 4P Framework was intended for lean decision-making. Oftentimes, when we have a large budget or funding, we mistakenly connect spending money to finding solutions. There is an inequivalency of spending more money means it was a better decision.

I believe very simply that better questions get you better clients and that, ultimately, those better questions create better. The founder often doesn't have the luxury of making this mistake. They have to get a lot done with a little bit of time and often a little bit of money. They ask a question that we should all continue asking you: How can I be more efficient, effective, and profitable?

This question comes up again and again: Who can I serve with excellence? Now, the founder has an additional question: Who do I love working with? We have to be careful running a business based on emotion, but this is a beautiful question. To go to work and think about what that does to your team and the interactions with the client. Think about what that does to your retention rate. Remember, sales is the transfer of enthusiasm from one person to another. If we're working with people we'd love to work with, you want to be asking the question: Where can I find 10 more of you? What would that do to your business?!

This is twofold. Remember, we always look at this internally and then externally. Internally: Who are the people I love to work with? Externally, I want clients I love to work with. The promise is the reason you get up in the morning. I see larger companies have either forgotten this or were never clear on this in the first place. It impacts the attrition rate of their employees, and it makes it difficult to attract and keep clients. I believe founders often have a more heartfelt understanding of the promise to themselves and their clients. With process, I see founders fly and fail because of a lack of process. They don't have operations, organization, or even write SOPS. They become a bottleneck within their own business and a barrier to their own success. With pricing, too many times I see founders very good at what they do with very poor sales. Pricing can be a source of anxiety for them, and the pricing is a reflection of their self-confidence. Instead of pricing me and reflecting on the value they add, they often give discounts and deals. One of my favorite quotes is, **"Don't decrease your price. Increase your value."** I think having strong pricing that makes sense for the market, the audience, and their abilities is a step towards better clients.

Let's look at several real-world examples.

The $7000 Chargeback

Is seven thousand dollars a lot of money to you? I worked with a founder who was earning just over $10,000 a month. She ran a consulting firm, accepting just a few clients each month. She had completed work for a client when she was surprised to receive notice that the customer disputed the charge. They said they weren't satisfied with the work they received. Unfortunately for the business owner, the client won the dispute. The settlement, a $7000 chargeback, was not only a large percentage of her income for the month, but it also froze her processing account, making it difficult to do business and destroying her confidence.

When she began working with me, I wasn't sure how to help her. I wasn't sure if I COULD help her. I started by asking questions. Then, I used an early version of the framework you learned in this book.

We worked on the People and the Process, which are the first and third Ps of the 4P Framework.

We analyzed her last ten appointments, creating a set of questions that would identify the right customer and avoid the wrong ones. Then, we wrote an agreement that protected the business and acted as a Service Level Agreement (SLA) for the client. Lastly, we made a payment schedule to make sure payments are completed in time with the work. We didn't have to implement any software or change her pricing. The end result was her first 5-figure revenue week and two back-to-back record-breaking months for her business!

Business Development or Sales Development Team

One of my biggest challenges was business development for a startup. I spent much of my first few weeks struggling to convert leads into appointments. I tried emphasizing our unique value proposition. I tried clever ways to explain the functions of our tool. One day, someone asked, "How will your tool help me do my job better?"

The answer was the Promise. The second P of the 4P framework. Where are you going to end up as a result of working with my company? How will buying my service impact your life or business?

The answer to that question became the catalyst for an over 85% increase in the conversion rate from contacts to appointments and a 90% show rate for appointments.

Being able to clearly and confidently communicate the PROMISE made the difference.

Full Cycle Sales Team

I led a small team of six outside sales representatives. The overall team was average, hitting 90% of our sales goal in some months and 105% in other months.

When I adopted the team, I had a mix of new and experienced representatives. Half were above goal, and the other half were underperforming. I asked myself how I could help the team succeed.

Here, I leveraged the PEOPLE and the PRICING. The first and fourth P of the 4P Framework. I paired the experienced reps with new representatives. I also created a simple pricing package—two simple options that reps could use to generate pricing on the fly. I'll admit I did a poor job of tracking the numbers. Looking at the big picture, I was able to accomplish two things: we increased the number of deals closed and we decreased our time to close. We also improved the performance of our reps, with the exception of one rep who decided to move to another role.

That is the power of the 4P Framework.

Consulting Agency

I had the pleasure of teaching a private workshop for Prima Business Agency. Our goal was to increase revenue using the 4P Framework.

Prima Business Agency Drives profit through productivity. As an operations specialist and scrum master, the founder works with leadership to help them work more effectively. She lives the idea of working smarter, not harder.

It is a phenomenal agency. At the time of this writing, they are helping one of their clients go public. How can the 4P Framework help a business that is already successful?

We found an opportunity when I asked, "Who do you serve with excellence?" We went through a few items. It was a strong list. But it was missing something. The Prima founders felt it was easier to ask, "Who do we NOT want to work with?" Sometimes, the contrast helps to create better clarity.

They said they no longer wanted to work with entrepreneurs. When asked why, their initial response was that they felt entrepreneurs didn't have any money. I challenged them. I have several friends with million-dollar businesses and only a few part-time contractors. So, it isn't the entrepreneur that is the problem. Why don't you like working with entrepreneurs?

They had the epiphany that their ideal client WANTS to change. They do not resist the support Prima was hired to provide. The demographics are the exact same as before they worked with our business. The difference is how they talk to the client and future client.

They wanted to attract clients who are doing well AND want to do better. There doesn't have to be a burning problem. Although they can help with extreme situations, their better client wants to reach the next level. This is the PEOPLE and the PROMISE realized. After this breakthrough, they decided to bring me back to work on the PROCESS and the PRICING steps of the strategy.

_____

_____

_____

_____

_____

_____

_____

_____

_____

_____

_____

_____

_____

_____

_____

CONCLUSION

The 4P Framework. Four simple questions.

That is all that separates you from here to your next level in business.

People. Promise. Process. Pricing.

Clarity in these four pillars impacts you as a leader. It improves your team's effectiveness. It influences conversations with your clients and future clients.

You picked up this book on a quest to be better. You believe investing in yourself and your team is valuable. And I thank you for allowing me to be part of the journey. This book will help you get a step closer. The answers are not in this book—this is the framework to get the answers. You can use this framework over and over again. Knowing the framework will empower you in every stage of your life, career, and business.

This book was written using the 4P Framework. It helped me find you, reach out and get this book into your hands. It has helped startup founders, commercial real estate agents, professional speakers, SaaS companies, agencies and more. These concepts are simple. But, they have been tested in challenging business situations.

Take some time to answer the questions you found most compelling. This could be a great workshop or even retreat. You will achieve a higher level of clarity, a deeper level of confidence, and be able to communicate more effectively. This will change how you interact with your peers and your team. It will change how you interact with clients and future clients. The result is increased revenue and improved retention. How big this change will be is up to you. It will be determined by your application of what you learn.

Of course, if you want help getting there faster or smoother, my team and I are here to help.

Email Bruce@newskillsnewyou.com.

Subject: Better Questions.

Thank you for the opportunity to serve.

Remember. One new skill will change your life!

Better Questions Toolkit

Linkedin/com/in/newskillsnewyou
https://www.youtube.com/@newskillsnewyou

Brittany Overton - Resistabl + Co

Resistabl + Co is a premier strategic consulting firm specializing in transformative sales and operations solutions for tech companies and ambitious organizations. We partner with individuals, teams, and enterprises to architect sustainable growth frameworks that evolve with your business.

Our holistic approach creates clear pathways to success by eliminating operational bottlenecks, optimizing sales processes, and building robust foundations for scalable growth through professional development, team optimization, and comprehensive organizational solutions.

Sales Optimization

We enhance your sales processes through tailored strategies that drive revenue and customer engagement.

Operational Efficiency

Our team analyzes and eliminates bottlenecks, ensuring smooth operations that enable growth.

Professional Development

We provide training and development programs that equip teams with the skills they need to succeed.

Strategic Partnerships

We build and nurture networks that foster collaboration and growth for all stakeholders.

Learn More Here:

https://www.resistabl.com/

Bruce Hill - New Skills New You, LLC

Build clarity, increase confidence, and practice more effective communication across your team and to your customer using the 4P Framework
Who can we help?

Startup Founder

You have an idea. You have a few customers. You are asking what's next. Maybe you have raised a round or are looking for early investors.

It is time to scale but every dollar counts. You need the 4P Framework

Professional Service Businesses

You get paid for what you know and the results you create. You're not a "sales person" and you really don't want to be. How do you scale your business while staying true to the identity it was built on. Use the 4P Framework.

Entrepreneurs

You are the business. You love what you do. You love to serve. You would do it for free. But you have to grow. You don't need to change who you are. You just need to change the questions you ask. The 4P Framework is for you.

Customer Success Leader

Your team is tasked with onboarding and serving the client. What you do is essential to the long term success of the business. How do we keep the clients we fought so hard to win?

The 4P Framework has training for you too!

Schedule a call with our team today!

Collin White - Blue Gopher

CONSTRUCTION DELIVERY SERVICE ON DEMAND SERVING GREATER COLUMBUS

A peer to peer delivery service designed to deliver tools, equipment, and materials safely to your job site or your home

How does Blue Gopher help?

Count on us daily to be a reliable delivery service.

Save time and money by reducing trips to the store.

We support projects big and small.

We are insured for your product's safe delivery.

Not in the Columbus, Ohio area? You can still support.

DOWNLOAD THE APP

https://www.bluegopherapp.com/

Meet Melissa – Fit For Legacy

Speaker, Storyteller, Changemaker

Hey hey, I'm Melissa Lee West, and I'm here to help you build, protect, and enjoy the legacy you deserve.

I didn't always know that this was my calling, but my journey has shown me how deeply important legacy planning is. I'm not just talking about life insurance or financial planning. I'm talking about the legacy you get to live and enjoy today, and the plan you put in place so your loved ones have peace of mind when life throws the unexpected your way.

Guidance for Families Building Their Legacy Together.

Support for Professionals Creating a Legacy That Lasts

Leaders and Entrepreneurs Who Want to Build a Community Legacy

Legacy isn't what you leave behind—it's what you live today. Let's plan for your future while embracing your present.

Learn more about how to create a Legacy that Lasts

https://fitforlegacy.com/

Sander Biehn - ReadyForSocial™

Empower Your Marketing and Sales Teams with Unified Social Media Strategies

Create high visibility, thought leadership, and drive more lifetime customer revenue.

ReadyForSocial™ social selling program creates opportunities for connection between sellers and prospects.

Imagine a Content factory that mines the best content, writes social captions in your voice with your messaging, checks it for defects with a proofreader and editorial specialist and then hands it off to your team for final approval. This is how ReadyForSocial™ works.

Our platform allows your approvers to approve or reject content and even tell our team what you didn't like about what we wrote. This allows us to get even better at creating what you want. Every step of the process is secure and auditable for future compliancy reviews.

Go ahead, do some peeking. Want to know how your team compares to your competitors on Social Media channels today? Let us create **a free Power Audit** for you that shows you on one simple page

https://readyforsocial.com/

www.ingramcontent.com/pod-product-compliance
Lightning Source LLC
Chambersburg PA
CBHW071202120626
46546CB00006B/2373